My

ADVENTURE STARTS HERE...

USA

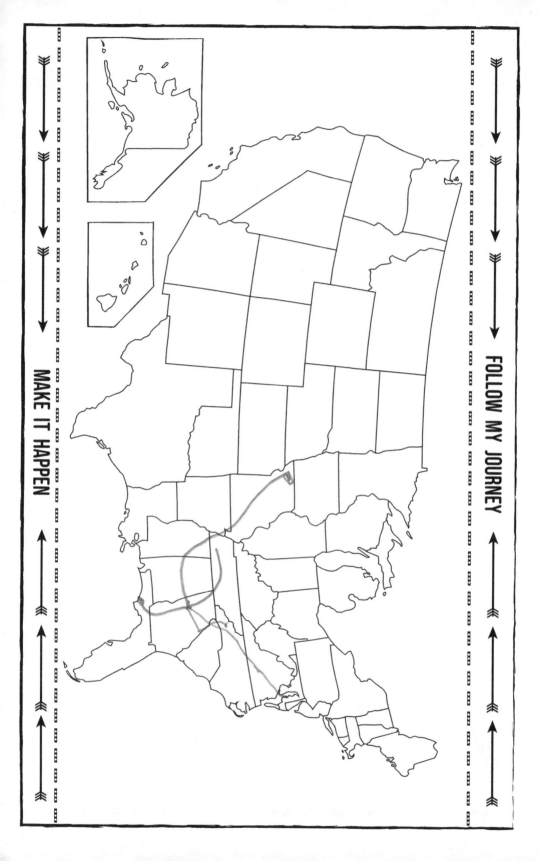

MAKE IT HAPPEN

Save the moments

MAGICAL MOMENTS:

DATE:

50 US States List

DATE of VISIT:
....

Alabama	AL	
Alaska	AK	
Arizona	AZ	
Arkansas	AR	
California	CA	
Colorado	CO	
Connecticut	CT	
Delaware	DE	
Florida	FL	
Georgia	GA	
Hawaii	HI	
Idaho	ID	
Illinois	IL	
Indiana	IN	
Iowa	IA	
Kansas	KS	
Kentucky	KY	
Louisiana	LA	
Maine	ME	
Maryland	MD	
Massachusetts	MA	
Michigan	MI	
Minnesota	MN	
Mississippi	MS	
Missouri	MO	

USA

50 US States List

State	Abbr.	
Montana	MT	
Nebraska	NE	
Nevada	NV	
New Hampshire	NH	
New Jersey	NJ	
New Mexico	NM	
New York	NY	
North Carolina	NC	
North Dakota	ND	
Ohio	OH	
Oklahoma	OK	
Oregon	OR	
Pennsylvania	PA	
Rhode Island	RI	
South Carolina	SC	
South Dakota	SD	
Tennessee	TN	
Texas	TX	
Utah	UT	
Vermont	VT	
Virginia	VA	
Washington	WA	
West Virginia	WV	
Wisconsin	WI	
Wyoming	WY	

ADVENTURE STARTS HERE...

USA

ALABAMA

Favorite memories

DATE:

Save the moments

„Veni, Vini, Amavi. We came, we saw, we loved."

ALASKA

Favorite memories

DATE:

Save the moments

"life is a journey, not a destination."

ARIZONA

Favorite memories

DATE:

Save the moments

ARKANSAS

Favorite memories

When we went to the arkansas - georda football game. and of the town there was very good pizza

DATE: Sep 26 2020

Save the moments

CALIFORNIA

Favorite memories

DATE:

Save the moments

„I never travel without my diary. One should always have something sensational to read on the train." - Oscar Wilde

COLORADO

Favorite memories

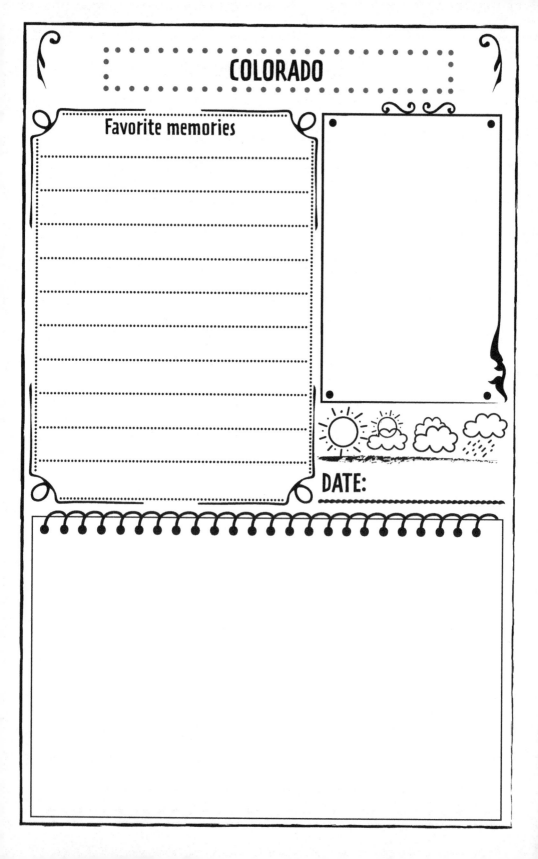

DATE:

Save the moments

"There's no way I was born to just pay bills and die".

CONNECTICUT

Favorite memories

DATE:

Save the moments

„Everything you do is based on the choice you make". - Wayne Dyer

DELAWARE

Favorite memories

DATE:

Save the moments

„One's destination is never a place, but a new way of seeing things". – Henry Miller

FLORIDA

Favorite memories

When we ~~memena~~
go to amelia
island.

DATE: eWefy yⱥ

Save the moments

„Life is either a daring adventure or nothing at all". - Helen Keller

GEORGIA

Favorite memories

I Live in georgia
I have alot
of memories

DATE: all o ustive

Save the moments

„He who would travel happily must travel light". - Antoine de St. Exupery

HAWAII

Favorite memories

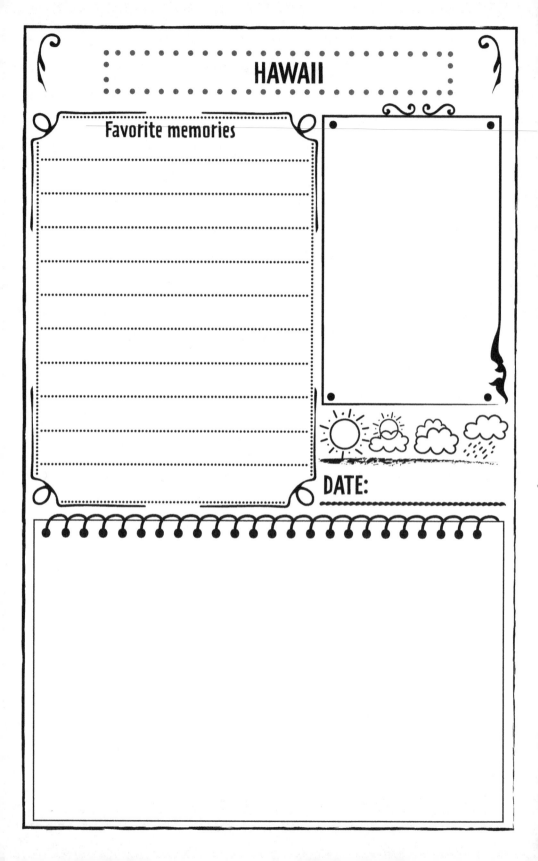

DATE:

Save the moments

„Travel and change of place impart new vigor to the mind". - Seneca

IDAHO

Favorite memories

DATE:

Save the moments

„Travel and change of place impart new vigor to the mind". - Seneca

ILLINOIS

Favorite memories

DATE:

Save the moments

„Dare to live the life you've always wanted".

INDIANA

Favorite memories

DATE:

Save the moments

IOWA

Favorite memories

DATE:

Save the moments

"The journey not the arrival matters". - T.S. Eliot

KANSAS

Favorite memories

DATE:

Save the moments

„Work, Travel, Save, Repeat".

KENTUCKY

Favorite memories

DATE:

Save the moments

LOUISIANA

Favorite memories

DATE:

Save the moments

„The life you have led doesn't need to be the only life you have". - Anna Quindlen

MAINE

Favorite memories

DATE:

Save the moments

„To Travel is to Live". - Hans Christian Andersen

MARYLAND

Favorite memories

DATE:

Save the moments

"Don't listen to what they say. Go see".

MASSACHUSETTS

Favorite memories

DATE:

Save the moments

„Adventure may hurt you but monotony will kill you".

MICHIGAN

Favorite memories

DATE:

Save the moments

"Better to see something once than hear about it a thousand times".

MINNESOTA

Favorite memories

DATE:

Save the moments

"Traveling - it leaves you speechless, then turns you into a storyteller". - Ibn Battuta

MISSISSIPPI

Favorite memories

DATE:

Save the moments

MISSOURI

Favorite memories

DATE:

Save the moments

MONTANA

Favorite memories

DATE:

Save the moments

„With the right mindset and spirit, only the sky is the limit".

NEBRASKA

Favorite memories

DATE:

Save the moments

„Live your life by a compass, not a clock". - Stephen Covey

NEVADA

Favorite memories

DATE:

Save the moments

„The goal is to die with memories not dreams".

NEW HAMPSHIRE

Favorite memories

DATE:

Save the moments

„Travel is never a matter of money but of courage". Paolo Coelho

NEW JERSEY

Favorite memories

DATE:

Save the moments

"Once a year, go someplace you've never been before". - Dalai Lama

NEW MEXICO

Favorite memories

DATE:

Save the moments

„I love the feeling of being anonymous in a city I've never been before".

NEW YORK

Favorite memories

DATE:

Save the moments

NORTH CAROLINA

Favorite memories

When we went to the polar express every year

DATE: dec 3 2016

Save the moments

„Then I realized adventures are the best way to learn".

NORTH DAKOTA

Favorite memories

DATE:

Save the moments

„Don't call it a dream... call it a plan".

OHIO

Favorite memories

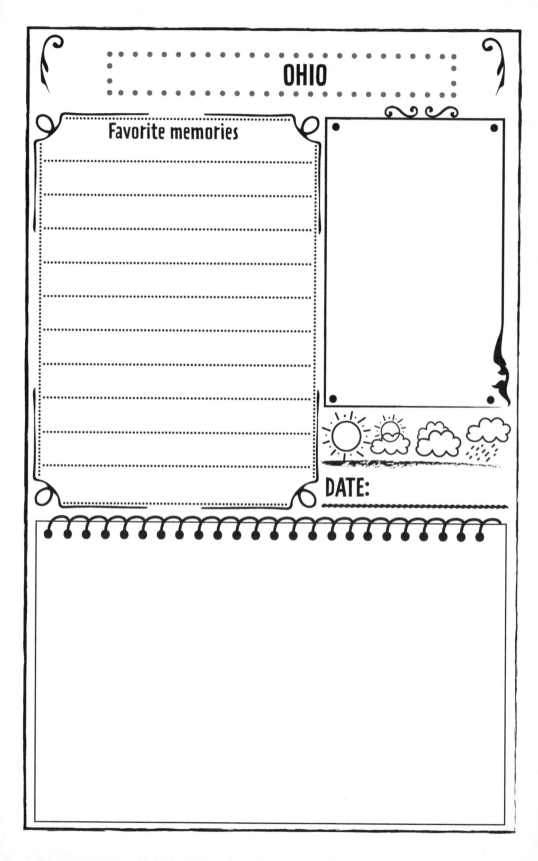

DATE:

Save the moments

OKLAHOMA

Favorite memories

DATE:

Save the moments

„Oh the places you'll go." – Dr. Seuss

OREGON

Favorite memories

DATE:

Save the moments

„I'm in love with cities I've never been to and people I've never met."

PENNSYLVANIA

Favorite memories

DATE:

Save the moments

„Take only memories, leave only footprints." – Chief Seattle

RHODE ISLAND

Favorite memories

DATE:

Save the moments

„The biggest adventure you can ever take is to live the life of your dreams."

SOUTH CAROLINA

Favorite memories

DATE:

Save the moments

"You can shake the sand from your shoes, but it will never leave your soul."

SOUTH DAKOTA

Favorite memories

DATE:

Save the moments

„Remember that happiness is a way of travel - not a destination." - Roy M. Goodman

TENNESSEE

Favorite memories

when we
went to the
memphis pyrimd

DATE: Sep 25 2020

Save the moments

„Blessed are the curious for they will have adventures."

TEXAS

Favorite memories

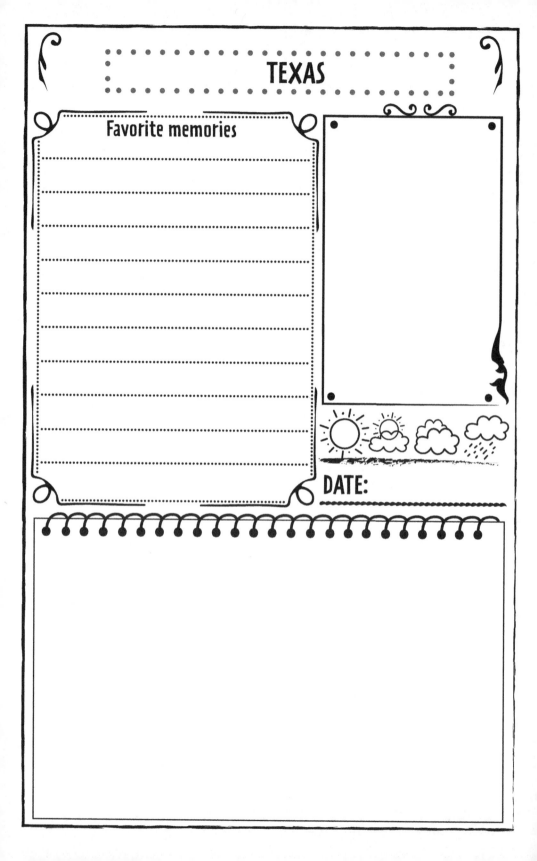

DATE:

Save the moments

UTAH

Favorite memories

DATE:

Save the moments

„Travel is the only thing you buy that makes you richer."

VERMONT

Favorite memories

DATE:

Save the moments

"Life is a journey. Make the best of it."

VIRGINIA

Favorite memories

DATE:

Save the moments

"A good traveler has no fixed plans and is not intent on arriving." - Lao Tzu

WASHINGTON

Favorite memories

DATE:

Save the moments

„The world is a book and those who do not travel read only one page." – Agustine of Hippo

WEST VIRGINIA

Favorite memories

DATE:

Save the moments

WISCONSIN

Favorite memories

DATE:

Save the moments

„All journeys have secret destinations of wich the traveler is unaware." – Martin Buber

WYOMING

Favorite memories

DATE:

Save the moments

"Travel. Because money returns. Time does not."

Save money

NEXT TRIP:

DATE:

NOTES

NOTES

NOTES

NOTES

Washington . d.c

date may 29 2021

NOTES

Parta rilo